ROMANS

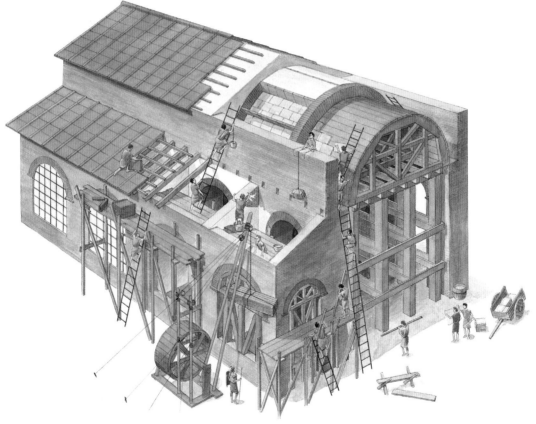

Written by John Haywood

Published by Brown Bear Books Ltd
First Floor
9–17 St Albans Place
London N1 0NX

© 2015 Brown Bear Books Ltd

ISBN 978-1-78121-226-4

A catalogue record for this book is available from the
British Library.

Designer: Mary Walsh
Editor: Dawn Titmus
Design manager: Keith Davis
Editorial director: Lindsey Lowe
Children's publisher: Anne O'Daly

Printed in China

CONTENTS

INTRODUCTION 6

THE ROMAN EMPIRE 8

THE ROMAN REPUBLIC 10

THE IMPERIAL AGE 12

THE ROMAN ARMY 14

A ROMAN FORT 16

TOWNS 18

BUILDING TECHNOLOGY 20

ROADS AND TRAVEL 22

FARMING & THE COUNTRYSIDE 24

TRADE AND SHIPS 26

THE TOWN HOUSE 28

FAMILY LIFE 30

FOOD AND DRINK 32

THE PUBLIC BATHS 34

ENTERTAINMENT 36

RELIGION AND DEATH 38

THE LATE ROMAN EMPIRE 40

THE END OF THE EMPIRE 42

TIMELINE 44

BOOKS 44

WEBSITES 45

GLOSSARY 46

INDEX 48

INTRODUCTION

The Roman Empire was one of the largest empires in world history. It was also one of the most successful and lasted for more than 700 years. Even though their empire came to an end 1,500 years ago, the Romans still have an influence on our lives.

Our alphabet was invented by the Romans. The languages of modern France, Portugal, Spain, Italy and Romania are all descended from Latin, the Romans' language. The English language also contains thousands of Latin words. The laws of many countries, such as France and Germany, are based on Roman laws. Many of Europe's great cities, such as London and Paris, were founded by the Romans. All over Europe, Roman buildings still stand to remind us of this great civilisation.

FIND OUT MORE

All kinds of objects that the Romans used in their daily lives have survived to the present day. Many of them can be seen in museums all over the world. You can find examples similar to most of the objects illustrated in this book in a museum with a good Roman collection.

HOW TO USE THIS BOOK

This book explores and explains the world of the ancient Romans. Each double-page section looks at a particular aspect of life in the Roman Empire, building up a fascinating picture of this important civilisation.

INTRODUCTION

Concise yet informative, this text introduces the reader to the topics covered in the section. This broad coverage is complemented by more detailed exploration of particular points in the picture captions.

ENLARGED ARTWORKS

Subjects that help to explain particular points are shown as enlarged artworks with an explanation of their significance.

SPOTLIGHTS

A series of illustrations at the bottom of each page encourages the reader to look out for objects from ancient Rome that can be found in museums.

THE ROM

The main reason that th were able to conquer su area was their well-discip highly trained army. The an attractive career for po Although there was the c being killed, the wages w and if they survived, retire soldiers enjoyed many priv The main strength of the a was the legions of infantry recruited from Roman citi

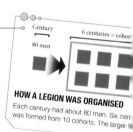

Century   6 centuries = cohor

80 men

HOW A LEGION WAS ORGANISED
Each century had about 80 men. Six cen was formed from 10 cohorts. The larger f

LOOK OUT FOR THESE

■ SWORD AND SCABBARD
The legionary's main weapon was the 'gladius', a short thrusting sword. It was easy to use in close combat and inflicted terrible wounds.

14

HEADING

The subject matter of each section is identified by a heading clearly displayed in the top left-hand corner.

DETAILED INFORMATION

From a well-organised army to the everyday life of labourers, a wealth of information helps to build a complete picture of the Romans.

ILLUSTRATIONS

High-quality, full-colour artworks bring the world of the ancient Romans to life. Each section is packed with visual information.

RMY

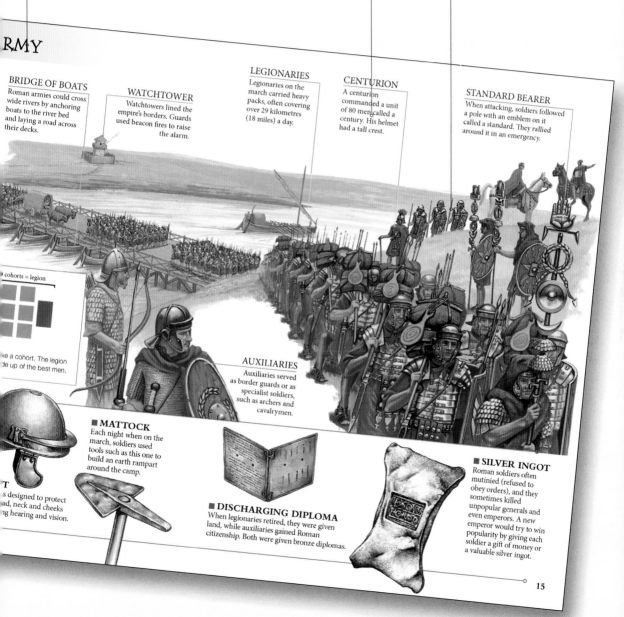

BRIDGE OF BOATS
Roman armies could cross wide rivers by anchoring boats to the river bed and laying a road across their decks.

WATCHTOWER
Watchtowers lined the empire's borders. Guards used beacon fires to raise the alarm.

LEGIONARIES
Legionaries on the march carried heavy packs, often covering over 29 kilometres (18 miles) a day.

CENTURION
A centurion commanded a unit of 80 men called a century. His helmet had a tall crest.

STANDARD BEARER
When attacking, soldiers followed a pole with an emblem on it called a standard. They rallied around it in an emergency.

cohorts = legion

ke a cohort. The legion de up of the best men.

AUXILIARIES
Auxiliaries served as border guards or as specialist soldiers, such as archers and cavalrymen.

■ MATTOCK
Each night when on the march, soldiers used tools such as this one to build an earth rampart around the camp.

■ DISCHARGING DIPLOMA
When legionaries retired, they were given land, while auxiliaries gained Roman citizenship. Both were given bronze diplomas.

T

s designed to protect ad, neck and cheeks ng hearing and vision.

■ SILVER INGOT
Roman soldiers often mutinied (refused to obey orders), and they sometimes killed unpopular generals and even emperors. A new emperor would try to win popularity by giving each soldier a gift of money or a valuable silver ingot.

15

THE ROMAN EMPIRE

In 396 BCE soldiers from a small Italian city called Rome captured the nearby city of Veii after a long war. Over the next 400 years, the Romans went on to build a vast empire that included many different races of people.

The Romans did not discriminate against people because they were of a different race or believed in different gods. They encouraged the people they had conquered to adopt Roman customs. They also rewarded loyalty to the empire with citizenship, and these people, whether they came from Africa or Syria, Greece or Gaul (modern France), thought of themselves as Romans. That is one reason why the Roman Empire lasted so long. It was even possible for a man from the provinces to become emperor.

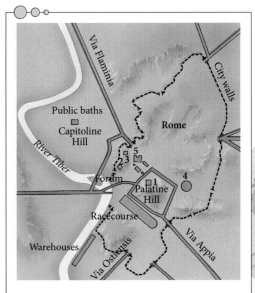

1 Emperor's palace
2 Temple of Jupiter
3 Temple of Juno
4 Colosseum (amphitheatre)
5 Senate House

CITY OF ROME

The first inhabitants of Rome were farmers who lived on the Palatine Hill around 1000 BCE. By 50 BCE, more than one million people lived in Rome. The centre was the Forum, which was surrounded by temples, law courts and palaces.

LOOK OUT
FOR THESE

■ FARMER AND WIFE
Wealthy Romans had portraits of themselves carved on their gravestones. This gravestone from the Rhineland shows a farmer and his wife wearing thick woollen cloaks to keep out the cold.

■ DACIAN
The Dacians were one of the last peoples to be conquered. This nobleman is wearing a Dacian pointed cap.

■ PORTRAITS
Many Romans, like this successful Italian baker and his wife, had portraits of themselves painted on the walls of their homes.

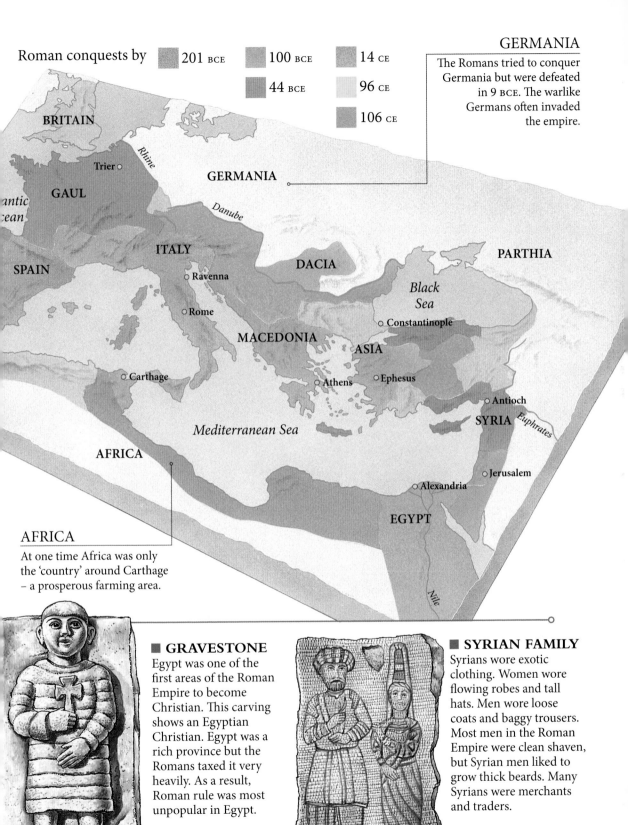

Roman conquests by

▮ 201 BCE	▮ 100 BCE	▮ 14 CE
▮ 44 BCE	▮ 96 CE	
	▮ 106 CE	

GERMANIA
The Romans tried to conquer Germania but were defeated in 9 BCE. The warlike Germans often invaded the empire.

BRITAIN

Trier ○

Rhine

GERMANIA

GAUL

antic *cean*

Danube

ITALY

SPAIN

○ Ravenna

○ Rome

DACIA

PARTHIA

Black Sea

○ Constantinople

MACEDONIA

ASIA

○ Carthage

Athens ○

○ Ephesus

○ Antioch

SYRIA *Euphrates*

Mediterranean Sea

AFRICA

○ Jerusalem

○ Alexandria

EGYPT

AFRICA
At one time Africa was only the 'country' around Carthage – a prosperous farming area.

Nile

■ **GRAVESTONE**
Egypt was one of the first areas of the Roman Empire to become Christian. This carving shows an Egyptian Christian. Egypt was a rich province but the Romans taxed it very heavily. As a result, Roman rule was most unpopular in Egypt.

■ **SYRIAN FAMILY**
Syrians wore exotic clothing. Women wore flowing robes and tall hats. Men wore loose coats and baggy trousers. Most men in the Roman Empire were clean shaven, but Syrian men liked to grow thick beards. Many Syrians were merchants and traders.

THE ROMAN REPUBLIC

Early Rome was a monarchy – it was ruled by kings. In 509 BCE, however, the Roman people overthrew the monarchy and founded a republic. Rome was now ruled by officials called magistrates. They were elected each year by a selected assembly of Roman men. Experienced politicians called the Senate advised the magistrates.

The Romans were often at war with their neighbours, and by 270 BCE, they had conquered Italy. Carthage, in North Africa, and the Greek states tried to halt Rome's expansion, but they were all defeated. By 27 BCE, the Romans ruled the Mediterranean.

As Rome grew more powerful, its politicians became corrupt. They gained power through force, not elections, and the republican system broke down.

TOGA
The toga was a semicircular piece of woollen cloth that was wrapped around the body. Only Roman citizens were allowed to wear the toga.

LICTORS
The consul was escorted by lictors in public. Lictors carried bundles of rods and axes called fasces. These were symbols of the consul's powers.

LOOK OUT FOR THESE

■ RIGHT OF APPEAL
Citizens were protected against wrongful punishment by a right of appeal. The assembly could overturn any sentence it thought unjust. This coin shows a prisoner shouting 'Provoco!' – 'I appeal!'

■ ROMULUS AND REMUS
According to legend, twins called Romulus and Remus were left to die by the River Tiber. They were brought up by a she-wolf. Later they built a city. Romulus killed Remus and named the city Rome – after himself.

CONSULS

The consuls were the most senior magistrates. They controlled foreign affairs and commanded the army in wartime. Two consuls were elected each year.

SENATORS

Only men with experience in government were allowed to join the Senate. There were 300 senators and they served for life.

TIMELINE

1000 BCE	Earliest evidence of settlement at Rome.
509 BCE	Rome becomes a republic.
396 BCE	Rome begins the conquest of Italy.
44 BCE	Julius Caesar murdered. Civil war breaks out.
27 BCE	Augustus becomes the first emperor of Rome.
116 CE	The Roman Empire reaches its greatest extent.
313 CE	Constantine becomes first Christian Roman emperor.
476 CE	The last Roman emperor in the West is deposed.

■ HANNIBAL

The toughest enemy of the republic was Hannibal of Carthage. This painted plate shows his invasion of Italy. In 218 BCE. Hannibal led an army of 35,000 men and 37 elephants from Spain; he won many battles but was finally defeated.

■ CICERO

We know what many famous Romans looked like because they had sculptures made of themselves. This bust is of the lawyer Cicero. He was one of Rome's greatest writers.

THE IMPERIAL AGE

After the Roman general Julius Caesar was murdered in 44 BCE, civil war broke out. It was won by Augustus. He made himself commander of the army and could make laws and reject any decision of the Senate. He called himself First Citizen. His successors used the title 'imperator' (commander) from which our word 'emperor' comes. This period of rule by the emperors is known as the imperial age. Though the emperors were sometimes cruel rulers, they brought peace and prosperity to the empire.

THE EMPEROR
After a successful military campaign, the emperor held a parade called a triumph. A holiday was declared and huge crowds turned out. Afterwards sacrifices were made to thank the gods.

LOOK OUT FOR THESE

■ MUREX SHELL
The most expensive dye of all was the purple dye that came from the murex sea snail. Senators were allowed to have a purple stripe on the edge of their togas but only the emperor could dress all in purple.

■ WINGED VICTORY
The Romans worshipped Victory as a winged goddess who brought success in battle. There were many statues of her, such as this one, on triumphal arches.

ENEMY CHIEF

Prisoners were dragged through the streets. The leaders were usually executed but the ordinary prisoners were sold as slaves.

CAPTURED WEAPONS

Heaps of captured weapons, treasure and even prisoners were carefully arranged to look like scenes from the battlefield.

AUGUSTUS

This statue shows Augustus as a soldier, the defender of the empire.

■ COIN

Special coins were sometimes issued to celebrate a new conquest. This coin announces the capture of Egypt by Augustus.

■ LAUREL LEAVES

Emperors did not wear crowns. Instead, they wore wreaths of laurel as a symbol of their power.

■ TRIUMPHAL ARCH

Great victories were commemorated by triumphal arches, which were decorated with battle scenes. Such arches were built all over the empire and many can still be seen. This one, at Orange in France, celebrated the defeat of a local rebellious chief.

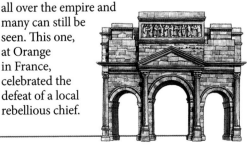

THE ROMAN ARMY

The main reason that the Romans were able to conquer such a large area was their well-disciplined and highly trained army. The army was an attractive career for poor men. Although there was the chance of being killed, the wages were good, and if they survived, retired soldiers enjoyed many privileges. The main strength of the army was the legions of infantrymen recruited from Roman citizens.

BRIDGE OF BOATS
Roman armies could cross wide rivers by anchoring boats to the river bed and laying a road across their decks.

WATCHTOWER
Watchtowers lined the empire's borders. Guards used beacon fires to raise the alarm.

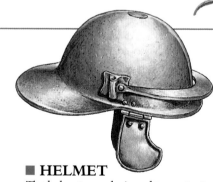

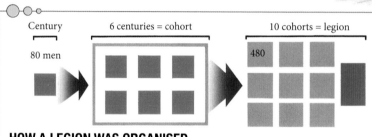

Century	6 centuries = cohort	10 cohorts = legion
80 men		480

HOW A LEGION WAS ORGANISED
Each century had about 80 men. Six centuries joined to make a cohort. The legion was formed from 10 cohorts. The larger first cohort was made up of the best men.

LOOK OUT FOR THESE

■ **MATTOCK**
Each night when on the march, soldiers used tools such as this one to build an earth rampart around the camp.

■ **SWORD AND SCABBARD**
The legionary's main weapon was the 'gladius', a short thrusting sword. It was easy to use in close combat and inflicted terrible wounds.

■ **HELMET**
The helmet was designed to protect the wearer's head, neck and cheeks without affecting hearing and vision.

LEGIONARIES

Legionaries on the march carried heavy packs, often covering over 29 kilometres (18 miles) a day.

CENTURION

A centurion commanded a unit of 80 men called a century. His helmet had a tall crest.

STANDARD BEARER

When attacking, soldiers followed a pole with an emblem on it called a standard. They rallied around it in an emergency.

AUXILIARIES

Auxiliaries served as border guards or as specialist soldiers, such as archers and cavalrymen.

■ DISCHARGING DIPLOMA

When legionaries retired, they were given land, while auxiliaries gained Roman citizenship. Both were given bronze diplomas.

■ SILVER INGOT

Roman soldiers often mutinied (refused to obey orders), and they sometimes killed unpopular generals and even emperors. A new emperor would try to win popularity by giving each soldier a gift of money or a valuable silver ingot.

A ROMAN FORT

Most Roman soldiers were stationed in forts close to the borders of the empire. Patrols were sent out from the forts to keep a constant lookout for invaders. Early forts were built of wood, but by the 2nd century CE, most had been rebuilt in stone. Each fort had a similar layout so that soldiers could easily find their way around. Legionary forts held about 5,000 men. Auxiliary forts, like this one, held only 500 to 1,000 men.

FORT DEFENCES

Fort walls were about 5 metres (16 feet) high and 3 metres (10 feet) thick. There were watchtowers at regular intervals along the walls. A deep ditch in front of the walls made it difficult for an enemy to attack.

STABLES

The Roman Army used large numbers of horses and ponies as mounts for infantry officers as well as for cavalrymen. They used mules to pull supply carts.

CIVILIAN HOUSES

Shopkeepers and innkeepers settled outside the forts, hoping to make a living selling food and other goods.

FORT GATES

There were four well-protected gates so that troops could march out quickly in any direction.

LOOK OUT FOR THESE

■ GRAVESTONE

This is the gravestone of Romanius. He was a cavalryman. Soldiers paid part of their wages to a burial club. The club would provide a funeral and gravestone when the soldier died.

■ STORES LIST

Some soldiers worked as clerks, keeping lists of men who were ill or on leave and food and equipment supplies. Instead of using paper, the Romans wrote on sheets of papyrus (made from reeds) or thinly cut pieces of wood such as these.

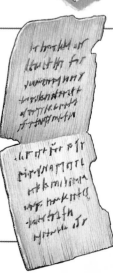

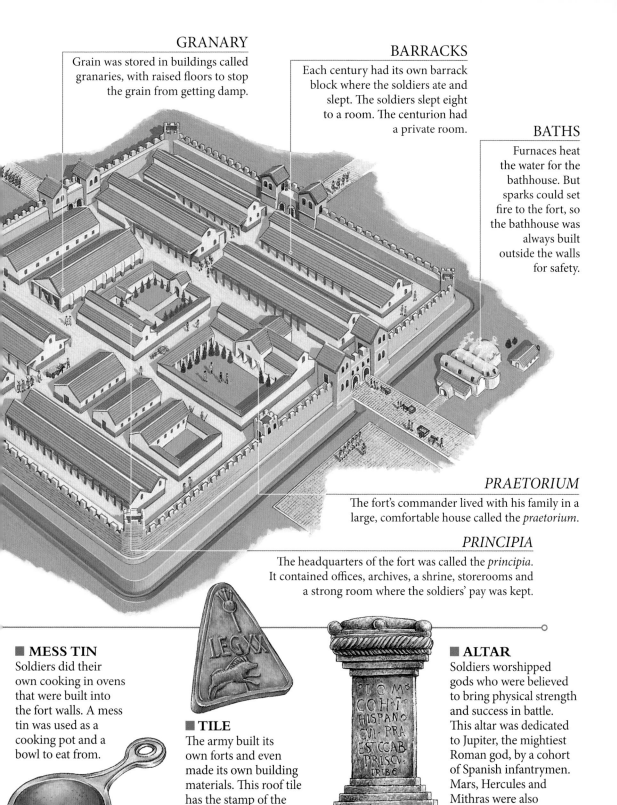

GRANARY
Grain was stored in buildings called granaries, with raised floors to stop the grain from getting damp.

BARRACKS
Each century had its own barrack block where the soldiers ate and slept. The soldiers slept eight to a room. The centurion had a private room.

BATHS
Furnaces heat the water for the bathhouse. But sparks could set fire to the fort, so the bathhouse was always built outside the walls for safety.

PRAETORIUM
The fort's commander lived with his family in a large, comfortable house called the *praetorium*.

PRINCIPIA
The headquarters of the fort was called the *principia*. It contained offices, archives, a shrine, storerooms and a strong room where the soldiers' pay was kept.

■ MESS TIN
Soldiers did their own cooking in ovens that were built into the fort walls. A mess tin was used as a cooking pot and a bowl to eat from.

■ TILE
The army built its own forts and even made its own building materials. This roof tile has the stamp of the 20th Legion on it.

■ ALTAR
Soldiers worshipped gods who were believed to bring physical strength and success in battle. This altar was dedicated to Jupiter, the mightiest Roman god, by a cohort of Spanish infantrymen. Mars, Hercules and Mithras were also popular gods.

Towns

Roman towns were noisy and crowded places in which to live. Although there were magnificent public buildings, most people lived in poor, overcrowded housing. Fire was a constant hazard and crime was common. There was no street lighting so most people did not go out after dark. Most towns did have a fire brigade and a police force, but neither was very effective. Road accidents and traffic jams were so common that many towns banned wheeled vehicles from the streets during the daytime.

Despite these drawbacks, the Romans thought that towns were the best places to live. They had the facilities that the Romans thought were very important in life: theatres, amphitheatres, racecourses, hot baths, taverns and take-away food shops.

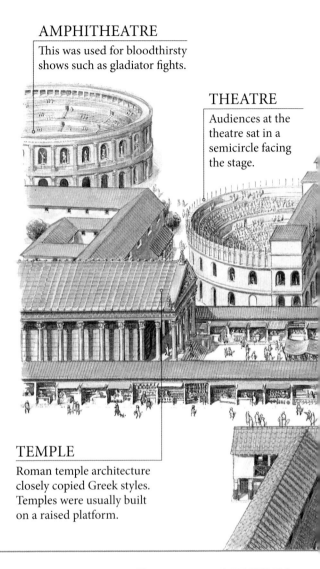

AMPHITHEATRE
This was used for bloodthirsty shows such as gladiator fights.

THEATRE
Audiences at the theatre sat in a semicircle facing the stage.

TEMPLE
Roman temple architecture closely copied Greek styles. Temples were usually built on a raised platform.

LOOK OUT FOR THESE

■ **PILLAR CAPITALS**
The tops of pillars (called capitals) were richly carved. The two main types used by the Romans were the Corinthian (left) and Ionic (right) styles. The Romans copied these styles from the Greeks.

■ **PUBLIC FOUNTAIN**
Only very rich people could afford to have water piped directly to their houses. Everyone else used water from the public fountains.

FORUM

The forum was the town's main meeting place and market square. The covered sides housed shops and offices.

BATHS

Every town had at least one public bathhouse; large towns had several. Baths were popular social centres.

AQUEDUCT

Aqueducts brought supplies of clean drinking water to the town.

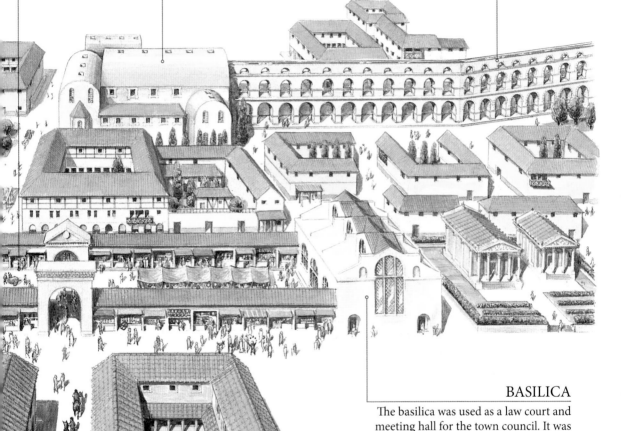

BASILICA

The basilica was used as a law court and meeting hall for the town council. It was always built next to the forum.

■ LEAD PIPES

The Romans moulded lead around wooden rods to make water pipes. However, lead is poisonous, so they preferred to use clay.

■ LATRINES

Very few people had toilets in their houses, so public latrines were built around the town. The latrines were connected to the town's underground sewers.

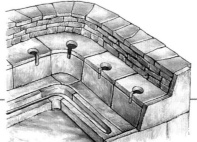

■ CITY GATES

Many Roman cities had walls to protect them from attack. However, strong walls and impressive-looking gatehouses, such as this one at Trier in Germany, were also seen as a sign of the city's importance.

BUILDING TECHNOLOGY

The Romans were skilful builders. Roman buildings were very strong and many are still standing today. Most Roman buildings were built of bricks and concrete. Stone was expensive, so it was often used just to decorate buildings. Roman builders were the first to become expert at using concrete and building arches. The Romans also perfected the dome. Thanks to these skills, the Romans could make their buildings spacious, with high roofs and big windows.

Some of the best builders and surveyors were in the army. In peacetime the army helped to plan and build whole towns. Also, town councils owned slaves, who were used as labourers on building sites.

WINDOWS

Glass windows were very expensive. Only important buildings had them.

ROMAN WALL

Two low brick or stone walls were built with a space in between. Then the space was filled with concrete. Another layer could be built on top after the concrete had set.

CRANE

Cranes lifted heavy loads. They were operated by slaves walking inside a treadmill.

LOOK OUT FOR THESE

■ ROOF TILES

Workers moulded roof tiles out of clay and baked them in a kiln. They stamped the tiles with the name of the factory that made them.

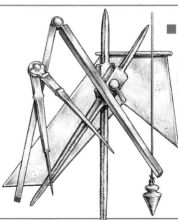

■ ARCHITECTS' AND MASONS' TOOLS

The tools shown here are a folding ruler, dividers, a set square and a plumb line. A plumb line was used to check that walls were straight. The ruler measures a Roman foot (29.6 centimetres; 11.65 inches).

CONCRETE

Concrete was made out of lime, sand and small stones. Concrete was very useful for building roofs. It weighed less than stone and could not catch fire like wood. It was also cheap to make.

ROOF BUILDING

Builders made a temporary wooden arch first. They laid a layer of bricks on top of the arch. Then they poured a layer of concrete over the bricks.

■ INSCRIPTION

Inscriptions are found on many Roman buildings. They explain when they were built and who built them. This inscription comes from a theatre at Leptis Magna, in North Africa.

■ TOOLS

This carpenter's hammer and bricklayer's trowel are almost identical to ones that modern builders use today.

ROADS AND TRAVEL

The Roman Empire had an excellent network of roads. The army built most roads, mainly because they allowed soldiers to travel quickly in wartime. However, the roads also helped trade. They made it easier for merchants to carry their goods around the empire. Some Roman roads are still used today. They are easy to find on a map because they usually run for long distances in very straight lines.

Sometimes wealthy people went on sightseeing trips, but most people did not travel unless they had to. They lived in the same town or village all their lives and rarely left it.

SURVEYING

The route was surveyed using a groma. It was difficult to use – it had to be kept perfectly level and even a breeze could cause it to be inaccurate. The route was marked out with wooden stakes.

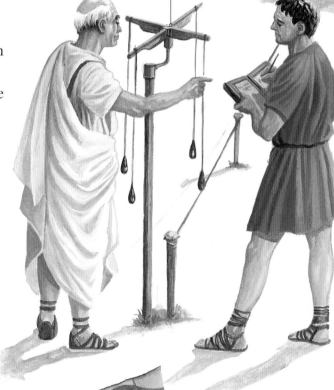

LOOK OUT FOR THESE

■ **MILESTONES**
A Roman mile was about 1,460 metres (4,790 feet) long. Each mile along a road was marked off by a stone. Like modern road signs, they told travellers how far it was to the next town.

■ **ROAD MAP**
This is a small part of a Roman road map. The map shows the roads and the distances between the towns and cities of the empire. Mountains, rivers and seas are also shown. Maps helped travellers to plan their journeys and work out how long they would take.

BRIDGE BUILDING

The Romans built strong arched bridges with stone and concrete. This bridge in Spain is still in use more than 1,800 years later. It is more than 45 metres (148 feet) high.

PAVING SLABS

The road was paved with hard-wearing stone slabs. The middle of the road was made higher than the sides so rainwater would drain away.

LAYERS OF PEBBLES AND GRAVEL

A layer of pebbles and gravel was rammed down to form a hard surface.

DIGGING

The Romans dug a trench 0.9 metre (3 feet) deep and 7 metres (23 feet) wide. They also dug drainage ditches alongside the road.

FOUNDATIONS

The trench was covered with sand and large stones. These were packed tightly to make strong foundations.

■ SLIP-ON SHOE

Horses wore iron shoes to protect their hoofs when travelling on roads. The shoes were held on with rope.

■ STAGECOACH

The Roman Empire had an official postal service. Stagecoaches carried mail and government officials all over the empire. Travel was slow. Coaches travelled only 40 to 50 kilometres (25 to 30 miles) a day and they were bumpy and uncomfortable to ride in.

FARMING AND THE COUNTRYSIDE

More than 90 per cent of the people of the Roman Empire lived in the countryside. Many were slaves who worked on the estates of rich landowners. Some were labourers who found work wherever they could. Others were tenant farmers (they paid rent for their land). Nearly all of them were poor. The slaves had the hardest lives of all and were treated harshly.

Country life was ruled by the seasons. This illustration shows some autumn activities on an Italian farm.

VINEYARD

Vines were grown to produce grapes for eating and for making wine. The Romans made wine by pouring grape juice into large jars and leaving it to ferment. The harvest was in October.

SHEEP SHEARING

Wool was the most important textile in Roman times. The sheep were sheared in April, before the weather got too hot. Sheep were also kept for meat and milk.

LOOK OUT FOR THESE

■ GRAIN MEASURE

Tenant farmers often paid rent and taxes in grain rather than money. This bronze grain measure was used by tax collectors.

■ PLOUGHS

Two kinds of plough were used. The smaller one, called an ard, could work only light soils.

■ TOOLS

Farm workers used iron tools. These are sheep shears, a sickle and a hoe for weeding.

PLOUGHING

Farmers ploughed fields before they sowed wheat and barley in November. Oxen were used to pull ploughs and wagons.

VILLA

The villa was the centre of a large estate. There was a comfortable house for the owner and his family, and a farmyard with barns, stables and workshops.

OLIVE TREES

Olives were an important crop in the Mediterranean. The Romans crushed them to make olive oil. The oil was used for cooking and as fuel for lamps.

SHEEP

Lambs in Italy were born in November and grew bigger in the mild winter.

■ HARVESTING MACHINES

Crops were usually harvested by hand using a sickle, but some large farms used harvesting machines like this one.

■ LABOURER

This bronze model from Gaul shows a farm labourer in winter clothes. He is wearing a short, hooded cloak, a tunic and leggings. Without waterproof coats or boots, outdoor work in winter was wet and cold. Farm labourers were poorly paid.

TRADE AND SHIPS

Trade was very important to the Roman Empire. Big cities such as Rome had to import large amounts of food from all over the empire. Luxury goods came from further away. Silk came on camel caravans from China, for example, and ships brought spices, jewels and perfumes from India.

Transporting goods on land was expensive, so most items went by sea. Merchant ships were strong and seaworthy but slow. Storms could be dangerous, and ships stayed in port from November to March to avoid winter storms.

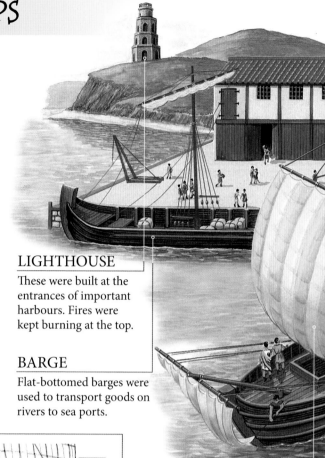

LIGHTHOUSE
These were built at the entrances of important harbours. Fires were kept burning at the top.

BARGE
Flat-bottomed barges were used to transport goods on rivers to sea ports.

GALLEY
The Roman Navy used galleys to patrol the sea against pirates. Oarsmen were highly trained professional sailors.

SAILS
Roman merchant ships were driven by a single large square sail. A smaller sail at the front was used to help to steer the ship.

LOOK OUT FOR THESE

■ BARREL
The barrel was invented by the Celts, a people of northern Europe. The Romans copied the design and used barrels to transport beer and wine.

■ AMBER
Amber is a valuable yellow-coloured fossilised tree resin (a thick liquid). German tribesmen collected amber from around the Baltic Sea and sold it to Roman traders. Amber can be carved easily into figurines. The Romans also believed that it had magical and medical properties.

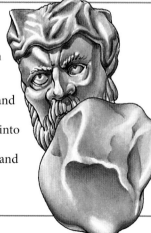

CORBITA

These were the most common type of merchant ships. They were slow and difficult to manoeuvre.

GOOSE HEAD

Ships often had a carved goose head, the symbol of Isis – an Egyptian goddess who was believed to protect sailors.

■ DOCKERS' TOOLS

These iron tools were used for handling cargo and opening packing crates.

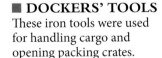

■ AMPHORAS

Amphoras were tall clay jars with pointed bases. They were used as containers for liquids such as wine, olive oil and garum (fish paste). Millions of amphoras were made, and most of them were thrown away after being used just once.

■ POTTERY

Factories making high-quality pottery traded their goods all over the empire. This pottery was made in Gaul.

27

THE TOWN HOUSE

Only rich people owned their own homes. This illustration shows the kind of house that a rich Italian family might have lived in.

Most townspeople lived in multistorey blocks of flats. Richer people lived in the lower storeys. These were built of brick and had large, comfortable rooms. Poorer people lived in the higher storeys. These were built of wood and the rooms were small and draughty. None of the flats had a kitchen, water or a toilet. The ground floor was rented out as shops.

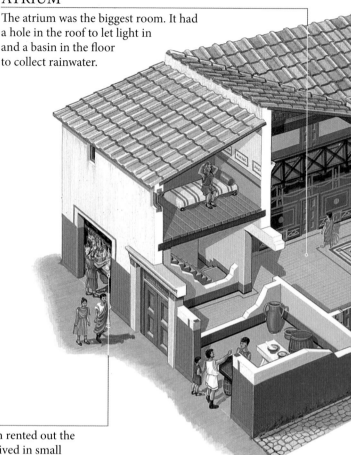

ATRIUM
The atrium was the biggest room. It had a hole in the roof to let light in and a basin in the floor to collect rainwater.

SHOP
Shopkeepers often rented out the front rooms and lived in small rooms above the shop.

LOOK OUT FOR THESE

■ SHRINE
The Romans believed that the family fortunes were governed by household spirits. Spirits called the Lares guarded the family while the Penates watched over the food cupboards. Every house had a shrine dedicated to these spirits.

■ FLOWERS
The Romans' favourite flower was the rose. Private gardens were planted with rows of rose bushes. The Romans grew many other flowers such as marigolds, irises and delphiniums. Peonies were also popular – they were believed to have medicinal properties.

WORKROOMS

Slaves' quarters and workrooms were at the back of the house.

PERISTYLE

The peristyle was an open courtyard with a covered walkway around the edges. The peristyle was laid out with flower beds, fountains and statues.

WINDOW

Windows were very small to stop burglars breaking into the house.

MOSAIC

Mosaics are patterns or pictures made out of tiny pieces of coloured tile, stone or glass. Laying mosaics was a very skilled job. This person is laying a floor mosaic. Mosaics were used in houses and in public buildings.

TABLINUM

The *tablinum* was the main living room of the house. It was usually built between the atrium and the peristyle. Guests were entertained there.

BEDROOM

Bedrooms were small and simply furnished.

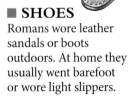

■ SHOES

Romans wore leather sandals or boots outdoors. At home they usually went barefoot or wore light slippers.

■ PORTABLE BRAZIER

Roman houses did not have fireplaces or chimneys. People heated rooms with portable braziers made of bronze. They burnt charcoal on the braziers because it gave off less smoke than wood.

■ OIL LAMP

Candles and oil lamps were used for indoor lighting. Oil lamps were made of pottery or bronze. They burnt olive oil. Candles were an expensive luxury.

FAMILY LIFE

Roman families usually had three children or fewer. Most parents were loving towards their children but they expected to be obeyed. Children had to grow up quickly. In poor families children had to start work as young as five or six. Richer children did little but play until they were seven. Boys then started school. Most left at 11 to learn the family business. Boys were considered to be adults at 14.

Girls were educated at home. They were taught how to run a household by their mothers. Most girls were engaged by 12 and married by 14. Marriages often ended in divorce. If this happened, the children always stayed with the father.

THE SON
Romans preferred sons to daughters because only sons could carry on the family name. If a couple was childless or had only daughters, they would adopt a son.

THE FATHER
Fathers had the right to whip or jail their sons. They could even sell them as slaves. Few fathers were that cruel, but they were always strict.

LOOK OUT FOR THESE

■ MODEL OF A BABY
Soon after birth the baby was wrapped tightly in bands of linen swaddling clothes. A baby's chances of surviving to adulthood were poor. Around half would die before the age of five.

■ TABLET AND STYLUS
Children learned to write using wooden tablets covered with wax. They wrote letters in the wax using a metal stylus (a pointed tool). The pointed end was used for writing. The blunt end was used to smooth the wax.

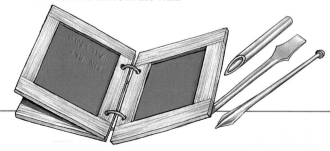

SLAVES

Household slaves were often well treated. Many were freed as a reward for good service.

WET NURSE

The wet nurse was a slave who looked after children. She washed, dressed and fed them, played with them and helped in their education. Often children saw their parents only at the evening meal.

THE MOTHER

With slaves looking after her children, the mother's main duties were managing the household.

■ TOYS

Roman boys liked to play with marbles. Girls played with rag dolls. Before marrying, girls gave up their dolls to show they were now adults.

■ SLAVE'S COLLAR AND DOG TAG

Slaves who were thought likely to run away were treated like dogs. They had to wear metal collars or name plates. These gave the name and address of the slave's owner. If they were caught, they were sent straight back home and punished.

■ RINGS

A couple exchanged rings when they got engaged. Late June was a popular time for weddings as it was thought to be a lucky time of year.

FOOD AND DRINK

Most Romans ate three meals a day. Breakfast was bread and fruit. At midday they ate a light lunch of bread, cheese, cold fish, meat and vegetables. For some, the main meal of the day was a three-course dinner served in the evening, but not all Romans ate this well in the evening. The poorest Romans did not eat well at all. The government gave them hand-outs of grain, which they made into porridge.

Most people lived in flats that did not have a kitchen. They either had to eat cold meals or buy hot food from the take-away food shops.

BUTCHER'S SHOP

Roman shops were small and sold a limited range of products. This butcher sells only pork, the Romans' favourite meat. The butcher advertised his shop by hanging a model of a leg of pork on the wall outside.

LOOK OUT FOR THESE

■ STRAINER

Food in Roman times was not as pure as the food we eat today. Wine usually contained grape seeds and pieces of stalk. Before it could be drunk, wine was filtered through a strainer. This was a large metal spoon with small holes in it.

■ MORTAR AND PESTLE

Every kitchen had a mortar and pestle. They were used for grinding herbs and spices to be used when making sauces.

KITCHEN

In houses, food was cooked over a brick oven. It was either boiled in a pot or roasted on a griddle (a flat iron tray) over the flames. The evening meal could take all day to prepare, and cooks were valued household slaves.

TRICLINIUM

The dining room of the house was called the *triclinium*. Diners reclined on three couches that were arranged around a low dining table.

EVENING MEAL

The main meal had three courses: a starter of eggs, seafood or snails; a main course of roast or boiled meat; and a final course of sweets and fruit.

■ GLASS FLAGON

After straining, wine was poured into fine glass flagons (large containers). Glass vessels like this were made by blowing a blob of molten glass into a mould. Glass was very expensive and broken bottles were collected and recycled, just as they are today.

■ SCALES

Shopkeepers used scales like these to weigh food. The Romans measured weight in pounds and ounces.

■ BREAD

Bread was sold while still hot from the oven. Bakers shaped the dough so that the finished loaf could easily be divided up.

THE PUBLIC BATHS

Romans enjoyed going to the baths. They were cheap to enter, so both rich and poor could afford to go often. Those who could spare the time went every day. Mixed bathing was not allowed, and men and women bathed in separate rooms. People did not go to the baths just to get clean. The baths were a place to meet friends and talk, gamble or play games. People could have a massage or go for a swim. Some baths had restaurants and libraries.

HOT ROOM
The heat and steam made bathers sweat, getting rid of dirt in the pores of their skin.

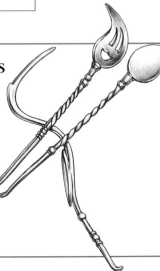

HYPOCAUST

A hypocaust was a heating system in which hot air from a furnace circulated under the floor and inside flues built into the walls, warming the room.

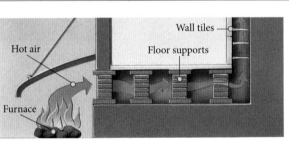

Hot air

Wall tiles

Floor supports

Furnace

LOOK OUT FOR THESE

■ STRIGIL AND OIL FLASK
The Romans did not use soap to wash. Instead, they poured olive oil onto their bodies. Then they scraped off the oil, along with any dirt on the skin, with a strigil. This was a scraper made of wood or metal.

■ TOOTHPICKS
After a meal people removed any food from their teeth with toothpicks. These toothpicks are made of silver. Romans kept their teeth white by rinsing with a mouthwash.

WARM ROOM

Before entering the hot room, bathers went to the warm room to get used to the heat.

COLD ROOM

Bathers went to the cold room last of all. Here they had a quick dip in a pool of cold water to give the skin a final rinse.

STEAM BATH

Furnaces boiled pools of water to fill the hot room with steam.

EXERCISE AND GAMING AREA

Before going home, bathers liked to rest or chat and play games with their friends. Some also did exercises.

■ SPONGE

Instead of toilet paper, the Romans used sponges on sticks. After use, the sponge was washed and dried so that it could be used again.

■ MANICURE SET

This pocket-sized manicure set includes a pair of tweezers, a tiny spoon to scoop out ear wax and a nail file.

■ TOILETRIES

Roman women used make-up and perfume. However, they paid most attention to their hair. Pictured here are a polished stone perfume bottle and a bone comb and hairpin.

ENTERTAINMENT

Most entertainment in the Roman Empire was free. Events were paid for by rich and ambitious men. By putting on a lavish show, they hoped to gain popularity and improve their chances of winning elections for positions in politics.

Though it was free to enter, people were not allowed to sit anywhere they liked in the arena or theatre. Front seats were reserved for the rich. Poorer people sat behind them and slaves had to sit right at the back.

Musical theatre and concerts were popular, but the best-attended events were violent ones such as chariot races and gladiator shows. The main event at gladiator shows was a fight between men armed with different kinds of weapons.

SPINA

The laps were counted from the *spina*, a building that ran down the middle of the racecourse.

CHARIOT RACING

Chariots were usually drawn by four horses. Races lasted for seven laps, with four chariots in each race. Each team of charioteers had its own supporters. They often fought each other and it was not unusual for dozens of people to be killed. Chariot races were one of the most popular forms of entertainment.

LOOK OUT FOR THESE

■ BOARD GAME

The Romans liked to play board games with counters and dice. Unfortunately, no rule books have survived so we do not know how the games were played.

■ ACTOR'S MASK

All actors wore masks that had exaggerated expressions. This one is the mask of a tragic character. Many people had to sit a long way from the stage, so masks were a way to help the audience follow the play.

RETIARIUS

The *retiarius* was a gladiator armed with a net and trident. He would entangle his opponent in the net before spearing him.

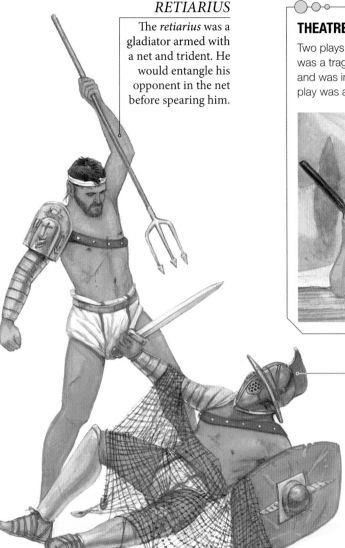

THEATRE

Two plays were shown at a theatrical event. The first was a tragedy, which had dramatic effects and music and was intended to make everyone sad. The second play was a comedy to cheer everyone up.

MURMILLO

The *murmillo* was a heavily armoured gladiator. He could be a dangerous opponent, but his weakness was that his helmet obstructed his vision.

■ GLASS TROPHY

This glass trophy was made to celebrate a victory by a charioteer called Crescens.

■ HELMET

This richly decorated bronze helmet probably belonged to a champion gladiator. The grille at the front protected the face.

■ MOSAIC

This mosaic fragment shows two men bringing in a deer after a hunt. Much of the countryside was still wild and there was a lot of wildlife. Hunting deer and wild boar was a popular pastime for country people.

RELIGION AND DEATH

There were many Roman gods and goddesses. Each one watched over a different activity of daily life. The Romans were afraid of their gods. The gods could easily be made angry and all sorts of disasters might follow. Romans believed they had to make regular sacrifices to the gods to keep them happy. No important decision, such as declaring war, would be made unless the Romans were sure that the gods would approve.

The Romans believed in life after death. They thought that a dead person's spirit was ferried across an underground river called the Styx to Hades – the land of the dead. Here the spirits were judged. The good went to heaven; the bad, to hell. A coin was placed under the dead person's tongue to pay the ferry fare to Hades.

ALTAR

Altars were set up outside temples. The priest placed the offerings mixed with incense and holy oil on the altar. These were all burnt so that the smoke could take the offerings to the god or goddess.

LOOK OUT FOR THESE

■ CREMATION URN

The Romans either buried their dead or cremated them. After cremation, the ashes were put in an urn for burial. Cremation urns came in all shapes and could be made of pottery, metal or even glass. This 'face urn' is from Roman Britain.

■ JUPITER

Jupiter was the ruler of the Roman gods. He was known as 'Best and Greatest'. Jupiter stood for good faith, honour and justice. When he was angry, he hurled thunderbolts and caused storms. His wife was Juno, the goddess who protected women.

MUSIC
Solemn music was performed before the sacrifice. At the kill the priest called for silence.

PRIEST
The priest had to make sure that the sacrifice was performed correctly. Any mistake would mean that the sacrifice would not be accepted by the god.

SACRED KNIFE
The animals were first knocked to the ground with an axe. Then their throats were cut with a sacred knife.

ANIMALS
A pig, sheep and bull were sacrificed at important ceremonies.

■ MARS
Mars was the god of war and country life. He was the guardian of Rome and would avenge any wrong.

■ MINERVA
Minerva, the goddess of wisdom, watched over writers, doctors, teachers, artists and craftworkers.

■ CHARM
People who were sick prayed to the gods for a cure. If they got better, people gave models of the sick or injured part of the body to the god to show their gratitude.

THE LATE ROMAN EMPIRE

In the 3rd century CE, the empire suffered so many invasions that it almost collapsed. It was saved by a series of soldier-emperors who restored the empire's defences. The rule of these emperors was harsh. Taxes were high to pay for the defences, and tax collectors were ruthless.

Christians had been persecuted in the early empire. But in 313 CE, the emperor Constantine became a Christian. He built churches and helped spread the religion. Within 100 years, most Roman subjects were Christians.

BUREAUCRATS
Officials were needed to collect taxes and keep records of spending.

WALLS OF CONSTANTINOPLE

The threat of invasion meant that cities were given strong defences. These walls were built around Constantinople (now Istanbul), Turkey.

LOOK OUT FOR THESE

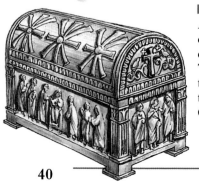

■ SARCOPHAGUS
A sarcophagus was a stone or marble tomb. It was often richly decorated. The cross on the side of the lid of this one tells us that it was used for a Christian burial.

■ SILVER VOTIVE PLAQUE
This plaque carries the 'chi-rho' sign. It stood for Kristos, the Greek name for Christ. Gifts of these plaques were made to the church.

CLOTHING

The simple toga was no longer fashionable. Romans now wore rich and colourful clothes.

EMPEROR

The emperor was a figure of awe-inspiring majesty. The Christian emperors claimed to rule the empire as Christ's deputies.

■ FLASK

Many Christians liked to visit the shrines of famous saints. They took flasks filled with holy oil home with them as souvenirs.

■ SILVER SPOONS

Christians gave presents to people when they were baptised. One of the most popular baptismal presents was a set of silver spoons. Baptism was an important ceremony. Christians believed it brought the person closer to Christ.

■ IVORY PLAQUE

Officials announced their promotion to new posts with these carved ivory plaques. This official has just been made a consul. Consuls were still important men, but they were not as powerful as they had been in the republic.

THE END OF THE EMPIRE

In the 5th century CE, the Roman Empire again came under attack from outside. This time there were no soldier-emperors to save it. The emperors had become weak and powerless figures. They were dominated by their officials and generals. The invaders were Germanic barbarian tribespeople. They did not invade because they wanted to destroy the Roman Empire. Instead, they wanted to live in it and share in its wealth.

The Romans gave the barbarians lands in which to settle. In return the barbarians agreed to help to defend the empire. This agreement worked for a time, but then the barbarians began to take more land. By 476 CE, they had taken over all of the western half of the empire. The eastern half survived for another 1,000 years and was known as the Byzantine Empire.

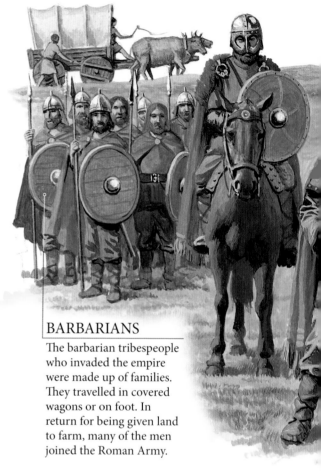

BARBARIANS

The barbarian tribespeople who invaded the empire were made up of families. They travelled in covered wagons or on foot. In return for being given land to farm, many of the men joined the Roman Army.

LOOK OUT FOR THESE

■ HELMET

Most barbarian warriors could not afford helmets or armour. This beautifully decorated helmet probably belonged to a king. He would have worn it only on special occasions, such as parades. It was far too valuable to wear in a battle.

■ JEWELLERY

Both barbarian men and women wore jewellery. Most jewellery served a practical purpose. Bow-brooches such as this one were used to fasten cloaks, for example. Decorated belt buckles were also popular. The finest jewellery was made of decorated gold.

CHIEF

The power of a barbarian chief depended on his skill in battle. Only a leader who was successful in winning wealth and land for his people could expect them to be loyal to him.

LANDOWNER

In return for giving some of his land to the barbarians, a landowner could expect to pay lower taxes to the government. He also hoped the barbarians would protect his estates.

ARMY OFFICER

Roman uniforms and armour had changed a lot since early imperial times.

■ CREMATION JAR

The barbarians cremated their dead. Then they buried the ashes in earthenware jars like this one.

■ DRINKING HORN

Drinking horns could not stand up, so a person had to drink the beer or wine all at once.

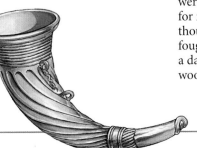

■ WEAPONS

The barbarians' favoured weapon was the sword. Swords were too expensive for most barbarians though. Most fought with a spear, a dagger and a wooden shield.

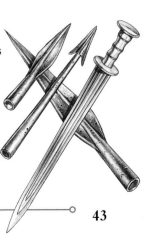

TIMELINE OF ANCIENT ROME

1000 BCE
Farmers who live on the Palatine Hill are the first inhabitants of the land that would become Rome.

509 BCE
The Roman people overthrow the monarchy and found a republic.

396 BCE
Soldiers from Rome capture the nearby city of Veii after a long war. Rome begins the conquest of Italy.

218 BCE
Hannibal of Carthage invades Italy with an army of 35,000 men. After many battles, he is eventually defeated.

44 BCE
Julius Caesar is murdered and civil war breaks out.

1000 BCE   **500 BCE**   **250 BCE**   **50 BCE**

753 BCE Romulus founds the city of Rome.

500 BCE
More than one million people live in Rome.

270 BCE
The Romans conquer Italy.

55 BCE
The Roman general Julius Caesar tries to invade Britain but has to return to Gaul.

27 BCE
Augustus becomes the first emperor of Rome. By now, the Romans are rulers of the Mediterranean region.

BOOKS

Chandler, Fiona, Sam Taplin and Jane Bingham, *Encyclopedia of the Roman World* (Usborne Internet-linked World History), Usborne Publishing, 2010.

Hawes, Alison, *What the Romans Did for Us*, Bloombury Publishing, 2009.

Hewitt, Sally, *The Romans* (Project History), Franklin Watts, 2013.

Marks, Anthony and Graham Tingay, *Romans* (Illustrated World History), Usborne Publishing, 2013.

Ridley, Sarah, *Life in Roman Times* (Everyday History), Franklin Watts, 2010.

Senker, Cath, *The Romans* (History Relived), Wayland, 2012.

43 CE
The Romans invade Britain, which becomes part of the Roman Empire.

3rd century CE
The Roman Empire is invaded many times and almost collapses. It is saved by a series of soldier-emperors.

313 CE
Constantine becomes the first Christian Roman emperor.

330 CE
Constantine moves the capital of the empire to Constantinople (now Istanbul), in modern Turkey.

395 CE
The empire is permanently split into East and West.

100 CE   **300 CE**   **330 CE**   **380 CE**   **480 CE**

116 CE
The Roman Empire reaches its greatest extent.

285 CE
Emperor Diocletian divides the empire into the Eastern and the Western Roman empires.

324 CE
Constantine reunites the empire.

380 CE
Christianity is made the official religion of the Roman Empire.

476 CE
The last Roman emperor in the West is deposed. The Eastern Roman Empire, known as the Byzantine Empire, survives.

WEBSITES

www.bbc.co.uk/bitesize/ks3/history/ the_wider_world/the_roman_empire/ revision/1/
BBC Bitesize Key Stage 3 revision pages on the Roman Empire.

www.bbc.co.uk/schools/ primaryhistory/romans/
BBC primary history pages on the Romans.

www.historyonthenet.com/romans/ romansmain.htm
History on the Net pages on various aspects of Roman life.

www.knowtheromans.co.uk/
Information about the Romans and their empire, with games and quizzes.

Note about websites:
The publishers have made every effort to make sure that the websites listed here are suitable for children. However, due to the changing nature of website addresses and their content, we advise that Internet access is supervised by a responsible adult.

GLOSSARY

Words in SMALL CAPITAL letters indicate a cross-reference.

altar A stone table on which sacrifices were offered to the gods.

amphitheatre A circular building where GLADIATOR fights took place.

archive A room where documents are stored.

ard A small plough for working light soil.

atrium The main room in a Roman house, which has an opening in the roof.

Augustus The first EMPEROR of Rome. He ruled from 27 BCE to 14 CE.

auxiliary A soldier who was recruited from the provinces of the Roman Empire. Auxiliaries served as support troops and were not as well paid as soldiers in the legions.

Baltic Sea A sea in northern Europe.

barbarian A word used by the Romans to describe the less civilised peoples who lived outside their empire.

barracks A building used to house soldiers.

beacon A signal fire used to give warning of an invasion.

brazier A portable heater used for burning CHARCOAL.

bureaucrat A government official.

Caesar, Julius A Roman general who conquered Gaul. He was murdered after making himself DICTATOR for life in 44 BCE.

Carthage A rich and powerful trading city in North Africa. Rome and Carthage were bitter enemies.

cavalryman A soldier who fights on horseback.

Celts A people of northern Europe. They were the ancestors of the modern Welsh, Irish and Scottish.

charcoal A black coal-like fuel made by heating wood.

Cicero A famous Roman lawyer and writer who lived from 106 BCE to 43 BCE.

citizen Two classes of people lived in the Roman Empire: citizens and non-citizens (sometimes called subjects). Citizens had more rights than non-citizens and could vote in elections.

cohort An army unit of 480 soldiers.

Colosseum A famous AMPHITHEATRE in Rome dating from 80 CE. It could seat as many as 75,000 people. Much of it still stands today.

Constantine The first Roman EMPEROR to become a Christian. He ruled from 306 CE to 337 CE.

Constantinople A great city founded by Emperor CONSTANTINE. It became the capital of the Eastern Roman Empire. It is now called Istanbul, in modern Turkey.

consul The most senior government officer in the Roman Republic. Two were elected each year. They lost power under the emperors.

corbita A Roman merchant ship that was slow and difficult to sail.

Corinthian column A Greek style of column that has elaborate decoration at the top, resembling leaves and flowers.

cremation Burning a dead body to ash before burial.

dictator A ruler with supreme power. The Romans appointed dictators to rule during emergencies.

docker A person who loads or unloads ships.

emperor A king-like ruler who held supreme power in the Roman state.

flagon A large container for drinks, usually with a handle and a spout.

forum The main market and meeting place.

Gaul A province that covered modern France and Belgium.

Germania A region that included modern Germany and eastern Europe. It was inhabited by war-like tribes.

gladiator A slave specially trained to fight in the AMPHITHEATRE.

griddle A flat iron plate used to cook food.

groma An instrument used by SURVEYORS to measure straight lines and right angles.

Hades The underworld or land of the dead.

Hercules A legendary hero of great physical strength. He became a god after his death.

infantryman A soldier who fights on foot.

Ionic column A Greek style of column that has scroll-shaped decorations on the top.

Isis An Egyptian goddess who was worshipped by sailors.

ivory A hard white material that comes from animal tusks.

Juno A goddess who protected women. She was the wife of JUPITER.

Jupiter The Romans' chief god and the husband of JUNO. He ruled over the other gods.

legion The main fighting unit of the Roman Army. Each legion contained about 5,400 soldiers.

Leptis Magna An important Roman port in modern Libya, North Africa.

Mars The Roman god of war.

mason A person who shapes stones for buildings.

Mithras A warrior god who was worshipped by many Roman soldiers.

monarchy A form of government in which the highest authority is held by a king or queen.

murmillo A heavily armoured GLADIATOR.

mutiny To refuse to obey orders, or to rebel against authority.

papyrus A reed that was used to make paper.

Parthia A powerful kingdom on the eastern border of the Roman Empire.

peristyle An open courtyard with a row of columns and a covered walkway around it.

province One of the regions of the Roman Empire outside Italy.

republic A form of government in which power is held by officers elected by the people.

retiarius A GLADIATOR who used a net to trap his opponent.

sarcophagus A stone coffin, usually with carved decorations or inscriptions.

sculpture The art of making figures by carving stone or wood.

shrine A room or container where sacred objects are kept.

sickle A cutting tool with a semicircular blade.

slave A person who is owned by another. Roman slaves had to obey their owners and they could not own property.

spina A building that ran down the middle of a Roman racecourse.

strigil A small metal or wooden tool used to scrape dirt from the body.

stylus A pointed tool that was used for writing on wax tablets.

Styx In Roman mythology, a river that was the boundary between Earth and HADES.

surveyor A person who marks where new roads or buildings are to be built.

tablinum The main room in a Roman house, between the ATRIUM and the PERISTYLE.

triclinium A dining room with three couches to recline on around the table.

INDEX

actor's mask 36
Africa 9
altar 17, 39
amphitheatre 18
amphoras 27
aqueduct 19
archers 15
arches 20, 21
architects' tools 20
ard 24
army 14, 15, 20, 22, 43
assembly 10
atrium 29
Augustus 11, 12, 13
auxiliaries 15

baptismal present 41
barbarians 42, 43
barracks 17
basilica 19
baths 17, 19, 34, 35
beacon fires 14
brazier 29
bridge building 23
bridge of boats 14
building technology 20
burial club 16

Caesar, Julius 10, 11, 12
captured arms 13
Carthage 9, 10
cavalrymen 15, 16
centurion 15
century 15
chariot race 36
charms 39
chieftain 13, 43
children 30, 31
Christians 40
Cicero 11
citizenship 8
city gates 19
clothing 40
coins 13
comedy 37
concrete 20, 21, 36
Constantine 11, 40
Constantinople 40
consuls 11, 41
corbita 27
Corinthian columns 18
countryside 24, 25
crane 21
cremation jar 38, 43

Crescens 37
crops 25

Dacians 8
dome 20
drinking horn 43

Egypt 9
emperor 12, 40, 41
entertainment 36, 37
exercise 35

family life 30, 31
farmer 8, 24
farming 24, 25
fasces 10
First Citizen 12
flask 40
flats 28
food 32, 33
fort 16, 17
fort defences 16
fort gates 16
forum 8, 19
foundations 23

galley 26
Germania 9
gladiator 18, 36
gladius 14
glass 20, 33, 37
gods 38, 39
goose head 27
grain measure 24
gravestone 8, 9, 16
groma 22

Hades 38
Hannibal 11
harvesting machine 25
helmet 14, 37, 42
Hercules 17
horseshoes 23
house 28, 29
household shrine 28
hypocaust 34

Imperial Age 1213
infantrymen 14, 16
invasions 40, 42
Ionic 18
Isis 27
Italy 10

jewellery 31, 42
Jupiter 17, 38

kings 10, 11
kitchen 29, 33

labourers 24, 25
Lares 28
late Roman Empire 40, 41,
    42, 43
latrines 19
Leptis Magna, Africa 21
lictors 10
lighthouse 26

magistrates 10, 11
Mars 17, 39
mattock 14
merchant ships 26
milestones 22
Minerva 39
Mithras 17
mortar and pestle 32
mosaic 28, 37
murex shell 12
murmillo 37
music 39

olives 25, 34
oven 33

Palatine Hill 8
paving slabs 23
Penates 28
peristyle 29
pillar capitals 18
pipes 18
plaque 40, 41
plough 24, 25
pottery 27
praetorium 17
priest 39
principia 17
prisoners of war 13
public fountain 18

religion 38, 39
Remus 10
retiarius 37
right of appeal 10
roads 22, 23
Roman Empire 89
Roman Republic 10, 11
Romanius 16

Rome 8, 10, 11 26
Romulus 10
roof building 20

sacred knife 38
sacrifices 12, 38, 39
sarcophagus 40
scabbard 14
school 30
Senate 10, 12
senators 11
sheep 24, 25
ships 26, 27
shops 19, 28
slaves 13, 20, 24, 29, 31
soldiers 16, 17
spina 36
stagecoach 23
standard bearer 15
strigil 34
Styx 38
surveying 22
sword 14
Syrians 9

tablet and stylus 30
tablinum 29
take-away food 32
taxes 24, 40, 41
temple 18
theatre 18, 36, 37
Tiber River 10
tile 17
toga 10, 40
toiletries 34, 35
tomb 40
tools 20, 21, 24, 27
towns 18, 19
toys 31, 36
trade 22, 26, 27
tragedy 37
travel 22, 23
triclinium 33
Trier, Germany 19
triumphal arch 12, 13

Veii 8
Victory 12
villa 25
vineyard 24

watchtower 14, 16
weapons 43
wet nurse 31